Real Estate Today, Seller Beware: Save Yourself Thousands of Dollars!

Susan Bulanda Copyright © 2013 Susan Bulanda

ISBN:148261121x
ISBN-13:9781482611212

This book in no way attempts to replace sound legal advice or replace a realtor, lawyer or any other professional associated with real estate. The intention of this book is to make sellers aware of the "tricks" or methods that some professionals use in negotiating a real estate deal based on the personal experiences of the author.

Introduction

Introduction

The following book is based on residential sales that my husband and I were involved with on the East Coast. Real estate transactions vary across the country due to laws and regional customs. Also the rules for commercial and land sales can vary as well. Regardless of the type of real estate deal, a seller must be careful. Most of what we explain in this booklet applies to all transactions.

I would like to make it clear that it is not the intention of this book to deny a real estate agent the right to earn a living, but we want to offer suggestions to the seller about ways to protect themselves from unfair dealings or to maximize what they can earn from their house. In many cases, real estate sales are the one chance in a person's life that offers an opportunity to earn a windfall.

This book will help a seller whether they use a real estate agent, sell a house on their own or use a limited service agency.

1 OVERVIEW

In today's real estate market sellers must be very careful to protect their investment and potential profit or to minimize their loss.

My husband and I have had to move frequently due to his job changes. As a result, we have had to buy and sell houses in four different states about 20 times. We have transacted houses in a normal market, sellers' market and buyers' market and each time have learned more about the ins and outs of selling and buying houses. What we learned can help you save a considerable amount of money.

It is important to keep in mind that in order for the real estate market to succeed, there must be a decent inventory of houses for buyers to look at which means that there must be sellers. If people are not selling and there are a lot of buyers, it can become a seller's market. If there are a lot of people selling and not a balanced amount of buyers, then it can become a buyer's market. A normal market is when there is a close balance between houses that are available and buyers, when the supply equals the demand.

The economic state of the country as well as local conditions and the availability of mortgages will also influence whether or not it is a buyer or seller's market.

What is very important to remember is that that many of the terms and conditions of a real estate contract are tradition rather than the law. This means that they can be changed or negotiated.

First and foremost, understand that not all real estate agents are equal. Some are fair and honest and others are not. The seller must accept the fact that although agents will tell you that they work for you, the seller, in reality they work first for themselves and often, next for the buyer.

Their main interest is in making the deal work and that usually results in give and take on both the buyer and sellers part. Unfortunate things happen when an agent is more interested in closing the deal rather than the seller's interests. The bottom line is that the seller must look out for himself.

Main Points to Consider:

Know the condition of the real estate market in your area

Real Estate contracts are not necessarily the law but rather tradition

All Real Estate agents are not equal

Real Estate agents often work for themselves first, and then the buyer

2 PICKING AN AGENT/AGENCY

With so many agency/agents available, it can be difficult to pick which agency/agent to use. However, there are a few things a seller can use as a guide.

Pick an established agency. It does not have to be a large or national agency such as Century 21 or ReMax, but the agency should have been in business long enough to have established a positive reputation. The advantage of using a large agency is that you have more agents to choose from and if you have to buy a house out of your area, you can get a referral from the agency to one of their branch offices.

Ask friends who have *sold* houses in your area who they used and if they were happy with the service they got and why. Get specifics about why they liked the agent.

Make sure those specifics are not because the agent was a nice person, but specifics about how the agent worked for the seller.

Drive through your area and see which agency/agent has the most signs up. While this is not a fool-proof method, you can assume that the agency/agent is aggressive about listing houses and/or that they have had referrals from satisfied customers.

When it comes time to select the specific agent within an agency, you must view it as if you are an employer hiring someone to work for you, and in fact you are, since you will be paying the agent. Agents are sales people and generally personable so they can talk a good talk. Do not use this to judge the agent, but rather judge by testimonials from satisfied seller clients as well as what specifically they can do to sell your house.

As for the testimonials, ignore the ones that are from buyers, and see if there are any from sellers. The reason is because almost all agents do a great job for the buyer. However, you are not a buyer, but a seller. You need an agent who will work for you, not the buyer.

Interview a few agents from different agencies so that you get a feel for what they have to offer. Pick an agent who will be on your side. This is hard to judge if you have not been involved in many real estate transactions, so it is best to shop before you agree to work with one agent.

What is important is that the agency has the ability to list your home with all of the multiple listing organizations in your area. There can be more than one listing service and sometimes the listing service may be limited to a specific geographical area. You want an agency that will list your house on all of the sites as well as on the web.

People who are buying from out of your area will view the houses on the web. What agents can do for those people is to set up parameters for the type and price of house that a buyer is interested in and send a list of the qualifying houses to the buyer. You want your house on that list if it meets the buyer's qualifications.

Lastly, it is important to keep in mind that your

agent/agency is most likely **not** going to be the one who finds a buyer for your home. Your agent will list your home on the multiple listing web sites and everyone, buyers and other agents will be able to view your home. Many different agents will show your house while it is available for sale.

You want an agent who is willing to host an open house for you. This is where the agency advertises that the house will be open for walk-ins for one day during specific hours. Some agents will argue that open houses are not an effective selling tool; however, it can generate traffic and possibly a sale.

Be wary of the agent who promises to get more money for your house than other agents you have talked to. These agents will promise a higher price to get you to sign a contract and then tell you that you have to lower your price later in order to sell your house. Pricing a house for sale can be tricky.

Main Points to Consider:

Choose an agency that is established

Ask people who have sold houses who they liked/disliked and why

Interview the agent as if you are an employer

Ask the agent what they can do for you to sell your house

Interview a number of agents from different agencies before you select one

Only consider an agent's letters of recommendation if they are from sellers, not buyers

3 THE CONTRACT BETWEEN SELLER AND AGENT/AGENCY

The sale of your house will involve two contracts, one between you and the agency/agent and then one between you and the buyer. The first contract between you and the real estate agency/agent can either cost or save you thousands of dollars.

Both of the contracts are typically generated by a real estate organization or the agency and contains terms generally favorable to them and is not necessarily the law.

However, when you sign the contract it does become a legal binding agreement between you and the agency/agent. This is why it is critical that you review the contract _before_ you sign it.

Real estate organizations write the contract to protect themselves. Not all contracts are the same and will vary from state to state and sometimes from agency to agency. Many contracts are written in favor of the buyer, not the seller. Here are a few contract pitfalls to avoid.

The duration of the Contract can depend on the type of market that exists when you sell your house. We have experienced contracts that required you to stay with an agent for six months and others that you could cancel at any time. If you sign for six months and find out a few weeks into the contract that the agency/agent is not good, you are stuck. It is better to sign for a shorter duration and then extend the agreement if you find the agency/agent suitable.

Be sure to understand the clauses in the contract that cover what happens if you fire your agent. Some contracts will allow you to terminate the contract but require that for a certain amount of time after, if you sell the house you will have to pay the agent's commission. This is not unfair because it protects the agent from people who will find a buyer as a result of a showing by the agent and then try to make a deal on the side to cheat the agent out of the commission.

However, before you sign the contract you can add a clause that details what will happen if you find a buyer on your own providing that the agent does not broker the sale.

If you have people who may be interested in your house, but are not sure, you can list them in your contract with the agent as being excluded from the terms of the contract. In other words, if a relative or friend is interested in buying your house, you can clearly list them in your contract as being someone who may purchase your house that was not brought in by the agent and therefore you do not pay the agent a commission for the sale of the house between you and whoever is on your list.

If this does happen, you can decide if you want someone other than your agent to handle the paperwork for the sale of your house. For example, you can use a lawyer or title company instead.

Main Points to Consider:

The sale of your house will involve two contracts

The contracts are not typically in favor of the seller

Set the terms of the contracts before you sign them

Contracts can vary from agency to agency and state to state

Reduce the duration of the contract in the event that you want to fire your agent

Set the terms of the contract to protect yourself if you fire the agent

4 THE AGENT'S FEE

Many agents will not negotiate their fee, but you should always ask. If the market is brisk, they may reduce their fee by 1% or so. One of the reasons an agent will give for not reducing the fee is that if the buyer's agent sees that the fee is lower they will not bring buyers to look at your house. We have never experienced this when agents have reduced their fee for us.

If your agent will not negotiate their fee, you can protect yourself by thinking ahead. Currently an agent contract requires the seller to pay 6% of the selling price of the house. The 6% fee is split between the seller's agent and the buyer's agent (note that this is custom and not a law). The seller and buyer's agent each get 1 ½% and each broker gets 1 ½%. So each agent makes 1 ½% of the amount of the selling price of the house.

Sometimes an agent for the seller will find a buyer for the house. If this happens, both the buyer and seller will be asked to sign an agreement that your agent can act as a dual agent, representing both the buyer and seller. Note that some states do not allow this. We do **not** recommend getting involved in an arrangement like this.

If you do decide to let your agent act as a dual agent insist that your contract be modified to reduce the 6%

commission to an agreed upon amount, which ideally should be 4%. This must be written into the contract between you and the agent **before** signing it. Under no circumstances should you assume that your agent will be fair and reduce the fee later on.

Another way to save yourself thousands of dollars is to change the contract to state that you will pay the commission on the **NET** sale of your house. Otherwise you will pay the commission on the **GROSS** sale of the house.

If you do not do this and you contribute any money toward the buyer's fees, such as part of the closing costs, you will also pay the agent's commission on that amount even though you never see the money. So for example, if you agree to pay $5000 of the buyer's closing costs, you will pay $300. (based on a 6% commission) to the agent for money you do not get. So in effect, you are reducing your bottom line by $5000 but you are still paying 6% commission on the full sale price of the house before your $5000 contribution to the buyer. What this means is that if you have listed your house for $200,000 but you gave a $5000 concession to the buyer, you have effectively sold your house for $195,000. Why should you pay 6% commission on $200,000?

Main Points to Consider:

Get the agent to reduce the percent of their commission

Do not let an agent act as a dual agent if it is allowed in your state

If you do allow your agent to act as a dual agent, have a clause in the contract to reduce the commission percentage

Make sure that the commission is calculated on the **NET** sale of your house

5 OTHER FEES

Sometimes an agent will neglect to tell you about the other fees associated with selling your house. It is important for you to discuss all of the fees in detail that you will have to pay. These can include a transfer fee or tax which can be, for example, 1% of the selling price of your house. You will also have to pay closing costs and title fees, as well as fees to your lawyer or title company. Every state is different. Even if the fees are listed in the contract, make sure you understand what and how much they are.

Some of the fees are an estimate at the time you sign a contract with the agent because those fees are based on the final selling price of the house. You will not know that until you settle on that amount of money.

In order to understand what you will finally get for your house, you must have a clear understanding of all the fees you will have to pay. The buying and selling of real estate is a big money maker, and is often the sole or major source of income for quite a few organizations or services, mostly all paid by the seller. Everyone wants a piece of your "profit" even though they have never paid a cent toward your mortgage and the upkeep of your house.

Knowing what you will have to pay will help you determine the lowest offer you can accept in order to at least break even. Remember, your real estate agent and the buyer are not interested if you lose money. You may take a loss, but the agent gets their full commission and the buyer gets your house for a less money.

Main Points to Consider:

Some fees are based on the final selling price of your house and cannot be calculated exactly until you settle on the selling price

Go over **in detail**, all of the fees that you are responsible to pay for

If you are paying any of the buyers fees, make sure that you know what they are (in detail) and why

6 PROTECTING YOURSELF

There are two things the seller hesitates to do because it costs them upfront but is one of the best ways to save money.

1) The best way to protect yourself is to get a real estate lawyer if one is not required by your state. Some states require that all real estate transactions go through a lawyer. While this seems like an added expense, I can tell you from experience it is the best way. The lawyer is the only person who will genuinely look out for your interests. The lawyer will take care of analyzing your contract with the agent and your contact with the buyer. A lawyer will also protect you if there is a problem at the closing with the buyer. Problems at the closing can become crucial since everyone wants to sign and leave. Poor decisions made under the pressure of the closing can be very costly.

   Most important of all, the lawyer will negotiate your contract with the real estate agent and represent you at the closing.

2) Get your own home appraisal on your house by

a licensed/certified appraiser. You can ask the mortgage officer in your bank for referrals.

Your real estate agent will do comparisons, or "comps" for you, but sometimes they will not be on target. Comps are a comparison of what similar houses have sold for in the past six months in your neighborhood. Your agent should show you what similar houses listed for and what the final selling price was. An agent will also show you houses that are still for sale as part of the comps. This will give you an idea of how the market is in your neighborhood.

What are not taken into account are the situations where people have sold their house for much less than it is worth. These "distress" sales are due to a number of reasons, such as, divorce, death, job loss, they owned the house all of their lives, paid little for it, do not hold a mortgage and therefore can take less than it is worth. Or some people are forced to move and must sell their house to buy another, and will lower their price. Recently, people have sold their houses to avoid foreclosure. The lower priced houses may have the same square footage, number of rooms, etc, as yours and normally would be valued at a higher price. If the lower priced houses (for whatever reason) are included in a comp, it lowers the value of all of the houses in the area based on the comps, while in reality your house may be worth more.

Agents want to turn a house around quickly, and may include as part of the comps local foreclosures and houses that are in terrible disrepair that are selling at a low price.

These houses should not be included in the comps since they are not equal in value to your house, but if they are included in the comps, the price of the house in disrepair should be adjusted to reflect the level of disrepair.

If an agent can convince you that your house is worth less and lists it for less; they may only lose a few hundred dollars in commission while you will lose thousands. When it comes to selling houses, your agent and the buyer will not hesitate to tell you to drop your price in multiples of $10,000. For example, if your agent talks you into taking $30,000 less for your house, they only lose $450 of their commission. You lose $30,000.

Another reason why you should have your own appraisal done is because your agent will tell you that in order for the buyer to be approved by a lending institution, your house must appraise at least for the amount of the loan. You will have no idea what your house is worth if you do not get your own appraisal. The buyer will have an appraisal done, but the seller is rarely given this document.

Typically an appraiser for the buyer will appraise the house at around the loan amount so that it meets the lending agency's requirements. You could be short-changed if you do not know what your house is really worth.

The real estate agent will tell you that the buyer will walk away from the deal if your house does not appraise for the amount that is being borrowed. This may be true if the buyer cannot afford more or the house does not appraise for the selling price. But understand that the house only needs to appraise for the amount being borrowed, so if your buyer is putting money down on the house, the down money is not included in the amount being negotiated by the buyer for the mortgage with the mortgage company or the bank.

However, the bank will not give a buyer more money than the house is worth. Therefore in a seller's market it is not unusual for buyers to put money down on a house to lower the amount being borrowed so that the house will be approved for the amount of the loan. For example, a buyer is willing to pay $400,000 for a house, but the house will only appraise for $350,000. In that case the buyer will put $50,000 down on the house which means that they only need a mortgage of $350,000 which is the appraised value of the house.

Knowing the real value of your house is important when you negotiate the price of your house with the buyer and can save you thousands of dollars. Some agents will give you a copy of what your house was appraised for by the local government for tax purposes. This amount is rarely accurate and is not the same as a bank appraisal and will not be accepted by a bank as an appraisal.

If it should happen that the buyers bank appraisal comes in lower than the selling price for your house and your appraisal, you can challenge it by presenting your own certified bank appraisal.

Main Points to Consider:

Most important of all
   Hire a Real Estate attorney

   Have a certified appraiser give you an appraisal of your house

Real Estate Comps are not reliable

Tax appraisals of your house are not valid for real estate purposes

You need a certified appraisal of your house in order to negotiate with a buyer

7 THE CONTRACT BETWEEN BUYER AND SELLER

This chapter will help you regardless whether or not you sell your house on your own, use an agent or partial service agency. In order to sell your house you must have a contract between the seller and buyer.

If a buyer wants to purchase your house their agent will present a contract to your agent. If you do not get a lawyer, be sure to go over every aspect of your contract by yourself first (if you feel competent doing this) and then with your agent. However, I cannot stress strongly enough that it will save you thousands of dollars by hiring a lawyer.

If you do not hire a lawyer, have your questions ready for your agent. Agents are required to explain the contract to you but keep in mind that they are not lawyers. Many contracts are written in favor of the buyer and all are in favor of the agency.

Homeowners can get upset at this stage of the process of selling a home because agents are required by law to present all offers to you, regardless of how ridiculous they are. Some buyers will try to offer you much less for your house hoping that you are desperate to sell. Expect this to happen and do not get upset. A good agent will tell you that this is a bad offer and to counter the offer, suggesting how much you should counter offer, but ultimately it is your decision.

The back and forth of offers and counter offers may go on for a few times before the buyer and seller agree on a price or one walks away from the deal. This can be a very tense time for both the buyer and seller.

The contract between the buyer and seller must be scrutinized very carefully, since the buyer may try to get terms put into the contract for their benefit. Frequently these terms are written by an agent who may not understand the legal connotation of specific words or phrases.

Watch for terms that explain what "conveys" or goes with the house, such as ceiling fans, appliances, curtains, window treatments, etc.

Watch for blank lines in your contract. Here is a sample of a blank line clause taken from the Virginia Association of Realtors Residential Contract of Purchase.

"Seller's and Purchaser's Option: In the event that the total cost of fulfilling seller's obligations set forth in paragraphs 13, 14 and 15 above exceed $_____ in the aggregate (the Remediation Limit) Seller shall have the option (i) to fulfill Seller's obligations fully at Seller's expense, or (ii) to pay or credit the Remediation Limit to Purchaser and refuse to pay any excess over that amount. If Seller elects option (ii), Purchaser shall have the right to either accept the Property in its present condition (in which case the Seller shall pay or credit the Remediation Limit to Purchaser at settlement), or to terminate this Contract and receive a refund of the

Deposit. If no amount is entered in the space in this paragraph, the parties agree that the amount shall be $1000. (Author underline) The Remediation Limit is independent of any obligations agreed to by Seller in connection with an inspection of the Property pursuant to a separate addendum to this Contract, or provision other than contained in paragraphs 13, 14(c) and 15 dealing with the right of Purchase to conduct an inspection of the Property."

Most people will glance over this or a similar clause and think that if the line is left blank then no money is involved. But as you can see, it specifically states that if you leave the line blank, you are liable for $1000. It is your choice to limit the amount to whatever you want, not what some organization decides. This is why you must be diligent about reading the contract and the best option is to have a lawyer who specializes in real estate and knows the contracts.

Also take note that many of the clauses for terminating the contract allow the buyer to get his "down" money back and no compensation is given to the seller for tying up the house and losing potential buyers while the contract is being negotiated. This clause can be negotiated as well so that the seller is not taking all of the risk by writing a contingency in favor of the seller.

Often a buyer will put a contingency into the contract. A contingency is a "if - then" clause. If _____ happens then we will do _____. In many cases a buyer will offer to buy your house with a contingency that says that they will buy your house only if they sell their house first. (**IF** we sell our house **THEN** we will buy yours.) This means that they will tie up your house while trying to get a buyer for their house. This could take months to accomplish.

If you want to accept these terms, you can put in a contingency on your behalf that says you will agree to the terms of the contract but that you have the right to keep your house listed, continue to show the house, and if you get another offer, your buyer has the *first right of refusal*, also called a "kick-out" clause. That means if someone else offers you equal or better terms for your house you will give the first buyer a certain amount of time, usually days, to purchase your house or the deal is off at no cost to you.

Main Points to Consider:

Hire a real estate lawyer

Read every word of the buyers contract

Watch for blank lines

Do not take your house off of the market while waiting for a buyer to sell theirs

Make sure your contract limits the amount of repairs you are responsible for (see next chapter)

Understand what conveys with your house and what does not – you have the say in this

8 THE HOME INSPECTION

When the buyer and seller have agreed on all terms, a smart buyer will pay for a home inspection. (Sometimes the contract will stipulate that the cost of the home inspection is divided 50/50 between buyer and seller.) The home inspection is when an expert will go through the house and look for any major repairs that should be done.

In our experience we have had home inspectors miss critical things, such as a rusted electrical panel with circuit breakers frozen in place, to home inspectors who could find nothing major wrong with a house and wrote things just to write something, such as rusted window screws and cobwebs on the siding.

"Used" homes will always have things wrong with them. Even buyers of new homes will have a "punch list" of items for the builder to correct. In general, minor findings should be ignored while major issues need to be addressed.

The lesson here is that the home inspection is not the final say. The sales contract can dictate that the seller can judge what is reasonable and what is not or that the seller will only pay a specified dollar amount toward repairs.

The seller does not have to make any repairs and it is up to the buyer to accept this or not. The home inspection report is open for negotiation, even though both agents may push to have the items taken care of to ensure the sale.

Keep in mind that some repairs may be necessary before a municipality will issue a certificate of occupancy (C of O) for a house.

Also keep in mind that while some repairs may be done by the home owner, the buyer will try to put in writing that the repairs must be done by a licensed contractor (this may be written in the real estate agency form, so watch out for this). Using licensed contractors will of course cost the seller more and may not be any better than a competent handyman.

The better way to handle this is to have it written in the contract that the seller will lower the price of the house to equal the repairs or to a specific amount, and let the buyer make the repairs or not. This will save the seller money in the commission fees if you have not written your contract to pay a commission on the net value instead of the gross value (the agent will argue with you about doing this). The home inspection is often another way the buyer will try to get more money from the seller.

Main Points to Consider:

Do not be frightened by the results of a home inspection

You only have to make repairs to meet a C of O –
Certificate of Occupancy

You can negotiate the items on the home inspection

9 THE FINAL WALK THROUGH

The final walk through is done right before closing to make sure that the house is in the same condition as the terms of sale. By this point any repairs that may have been done as a result of the home inspection should have been made and the buyer will check to insure that they were done. Sometimes the buyer will require copies of the bills.

What some buyers do at the final walk through or at the closing is to demand that "newly found" items be paid for by the sellers. They feel that the seller will not walk away from the deal at this point and that they can get more money out of the seller.

You have to decide if you will walk away or not and be prepared to do so. However, never forget that the buyer has paid for the home inspection; they have money invested in the deal and are less likely to walk away over last minute manipulations to get more money. They count on the seller panicking and giving in, but it works both ways.

Main Points to Consider:

Do your own final inspection to make sure that everything is the same

Do not be frightened or upset over last minute demands by the buyer

You do not have to accept them

10 REAL ESTATE TACTICS TO WATCH FOR

One of the more common tactics that we have experienced is how the agent will calculate a work sheet to show you what you can expect to get from the sale of your house. They will start with the price you are asking for the house and subtract what you owe on the house plus some fees and give you the bottom line. For example, if you want to sell your house for $200,000 and you owe $120,000, less $1000 in "fees" minus the commission of $12,000 equals $67000. ($200,000 - $120,000 - $1000 - $12,000 = $67,000.)   The agent will tell you that if you sell your house for $200,000 you will get a check for $67,000. This is not the correct way to calculate what you will earn from the sale of your house.

Incorrect calculation:

Sale Price of the house:	$ 200,000
Balance of your Mtg:	- 120,000
Fees:	1,000
Commission:	12,000
	————
Check to you:	$67,000

Correct calculation:

The Sale price of your house, $200,000, minus what you **Paid** for the house $150,000 minus any fees and commissions.

Sale Price of the House:	$200,000
What you Paid for the house:	- 150,000
Fees:	- 1,000
Commission:	- 12,000
	_____
Profit to you:	$37,000

The balance that you owe on the house represents the money you put down on the house plus the principal that you paid down through your loan. This is all money that came "out of your pocket" and should not be calculated as part of your "profit." The only profit that you will make on your house is the value it went up during the time you owned it which will be reflected by the current market price when you sell it. In reality if you sell your house for $200,000, and paid $150,000 which equals $50,000 profit, less the agent's fees and other fees, your profit is $37,000.

This is quite a bit different from the first example. In reality you will get a check for $67,000 but some of that money is your money, equity you put into your house, and should not be counted as profit.

The initial worksheet as explained above will rarely be the final amount that you get, because it is based on the starting asking price of your house. By keeping a piece of paper with the correct numbers on it, you can quickly recalculate what your final profit/loss will be based on the amount of your final selling price. This will help you determine what the final numbers will be.

If the value of your house went down, then you will take a loss, even though you may get money back from your sale because of what you paid down on your house.

Since tax laws change every year, be sure to ask your C.P.A. how the sale of your house, either with a profit or loss, will affect your tax return, (such as capital gains/loss). The way the sale of your house affects your tax return will _not_ be reflected in your real estate deal or worksheet.

When an agent first presents an offer to a seller, they may provide a letter of credit from a bank on the behalf of the buyer. The letter will usually state that the buyer is qualified for a loan in a named amount. What the seller must recognize is that often an agent or the buyer will ask the bank to provide a letter at the exact, _lower_ amount that the buyer wants to offer for the house. Their hope is that the seller will think that the buyer is not qualified for more, when in reality the buyer may be qualified for a higher loan amount. This is a ruse to get the seller to come down in their price to one that the buyer wants to pay.

The seller's agent may try to convince the seller that in order to sell their house they must meet certain customary practices, such as paying all of or part of the buyers closing costs. If the seller wants to do this, offer to pay for part of the closing costs, not all of the costs.

Under no circumstances should you agree to pay a percent of the selling price. This is one way fees can be hidden until the last minute. Always name a dollar amount.

If your contract is not based on the net sale of your

house but rather on the gross sale, the best option is to lower the price of the house so that you do not pay commission on these fees.

Sometimes a real estate agent will tell you that the lending entity requires the seller to pay for all or part of the closing costs. This can be true with some government funded loans, such as a VA loan, but be sure to find out since these laws can change. And keep in mind that you do not have to agree to pay these fees.

The seller's agent will often give the seller a tale of woe about how poor the buyer is and that they are just starting out, and really want your house. If you feel like being a benevolent philanthropist, you can buy the story. In our experience, we have never heard a reverse story about the poor senior citizen who is giving up their retirement investment or the poor seller who has to take a loss on their hard earned investment and need the money from their house to get the next one. The issue should be that if the buyer cannot afford your house or any house, they should not be in the market to buy one.

Often the seller's agent will ask the seller to repaint their house, (inside and/or out) put in new carpets or do other repairs to make the house more sellable. Sometimes this is necessary, but from our experience, and we have looked at hundreds of houses over the years, most houses on the market are not upgraded.

It is always a good idea to schedule viewings of houses comparable to yours in your area to see exactly what your competition looks like.

Agents will tell the seller to upgrade because buyers often expect the house to be in perfect condition and do not feel that they should offer you more for improvements done to a house. Upgrades rarely make a house sell for more money. However, if your house is in disrepair it will not sell or you will get a low offer to start with. The seller must decide what is reasonable and what is not.

Keep in mind that agents make money by the volume of sales they make, so whatever can be done to speed up turn-around increases volume. Upgrades do not profit the seller, but does profit the agent by increasing volume.

While your house is on the market, you will hear all of the negative feedback about your house. Comments such as the rooms are too small, it only has one garage, and the yard is too big/small, etc.

The most common one is that it is "dated," which typically means that the buyer has watched TV shows and thinks that all houses have to have the latest gadgets, appliances and whatever countertops are in fashion at the time. Realistically, many if not most of the houses on the market do not have all of the latest upgrades.

Never forget that when you hear the negative comments about your house, the person who likes your house will buy it and the ones that do not like your house are the ones leaving the negative comments. Buyers are fickle and it is hard to predict what people like and do not like. It is important to remember that you cannot please everyone. However, if you constantly hear the same comment from a good number of lookers, then you should give it consideration.

Main Points to Consider:

Understand how to calculate your final profit/loss

The buyer's letter of credit may reflect the low price the buyer wants to pay for your house and not what they are qualified to borrow

The real estate agent may try to play on your emotions to get you to take less for your house

View similar houses in your area that are for sale to see what your competition is like

Do not be upset by negative feedback

Do not make major repairs just to make your house more sellable

Do make necessary repairs, using common sense

11 THE HUD STATEMENT

At the closing or just before, the buyer and seller will get a HUD statement from their lawyer or title company.

Be sure to read every line of the HUD carefully. It has been our experience that a payoff to the buyer's credit card company was included in the closing costs and was originally labeled as closing costs and not as a credit card payoff. (We did not pay it.) What that means is that the seller pays the buyers credit card debt in order for the seller to meet the loan requirements. (This can be legal with certain government backed loans.) Make sure that if you verbally agree to consider paying any or all of the closing costs for a buyer, that your agent or ideally your lawyer explains just what those expenses will be **before you sign an agreement**.

Typically some of the fees that are involved with the closing can be negotiated. Your lawyer or title company should get fees removed or reduced for you. We have always gotten some fees reduced or removed.

Main Points to Consider:

Read every line of the HUD statement BEFORE you sign it

Question all fees -- Many fees from title companies, banks, etc can be reduced or eliminated

12 FINAL ADVICE

The two hardest things about selling a house are:

First, protecting yourself to get the best deal you can. The only people who will sincerely work for you are your title company or lawyer and you.

The second most difficult thing about selling a house is your emotional attachment to your house. Because of their emotional attachment to their home people will be offended when potential buyers do not like it.

To make the transaction as pleasant as possible, a seller must try to keep their personal feelings out of the deal. This of course is easier said than done. By protecting yourself and thinking ahead, you can make selling a home a pleasant and financially rewarding experience.

Main Points to Consider:

Protect yourself – get a lawyer before you find an agent

Do not get upset when buyers do not like your house, it only means it is not their style

ABOUT THE AUTHOR

Susan Bulanda, M.A.,C.A.B.C is an award winning author of books and articles. She is an adjunct professor at Kutztown University where she developed two programs for students who want to become dog trainers and canine behavior consultants. She holds a Bachelors Degree from William Paterson University and a Masters Degree from Monmouth University.

Ms. Bulanda is a certified animal behavior consultant and an expert in canine search and rescue.

Other Books by Susan Bulanda:

READY! Training the Search and Rescue Dog

Faithful Friends: Holocaust Survivor's Stories of the Pets who Gave Them Comfort, Suffered Alongside Them and Waited for Their Return

Boston Terriers

Ready to Serve, Ready to Save: Strategies of Real-Life Search & Rescue Missions

God's Creatures: A Biblical View of Animals

Scenting on the Wind: Scent Work for Hunting Dogs

For More Information visit: www.sbulanda.com